Praise for Amanda H

"Amanda Huggins' poems [...] They touch the heart through the honesty and precision of their intense personal insights, together with their striking harmonic beauty." **Adam Feinstein, author of** *Pablo Neruda: A Passion for Life*

"She pulls off one of the most difficult feats in poetry, the camera of commentary. The reader sees and feels everything; the tiniest details, both in close-up and widescreen." **Ralph Dartford, author of** *Hidden Music*

"*The Collective Nouns for Birds* was awarded the hotly contested Saboteur Award, a fine accolade for this collection of free verse poems which roam round family, community, and coming of age with skill and aplomb ... Here is a narrative voice moving not just from one location to another but from the aspirations and romantic imaginings of adolescence to the disillusionment of adult life ... We find the poet always watching and waiting, eager to share familiar and new worlds with her reader ... a travel writer bringing her acute powers of observation, her detachment and her passion to the medium of poetry, with memorable effect." **Hannah Stone, author of** *Swn y Morloi*, **and** *Reflections: a poet-theologian in Lockdown Leeds*

"Huggins' poems are structurally sharp, with each word earning its place. But there's equally a warm playfulness in many poems, which the reader can imagine being delivered with a wink ... *The Collective Nouns for Birds* is a compelling collection, carefully stitched with that thread of the sea, and mermaids, birds, imagination, memory, loss, place and relationships ... It would be difficult for any reader not to make some kind of personal connection with these poems ... a collection which will linger sweetly in the heart and mind." **Natalie Scott, author of** *Rare Birds: Voices of Holloway Prison*

"Naturally, I was drawn to Amanda Huggins' avian gathering, which also features 'stranded mermaids', 'jellyfish in puffball skirts' and teenage girls who anticipate leaving their 'one-trick town': 'We each hold the new knowing close to our ribs / and don't speak of it, just in case it isn't true.' As well as 'The New Knowing' and the others quoted from above, I also especially liked 'A Heavy, Haloed Star' and 'Violet Cream'." **John McCullough, author of** *Reckless Paper Birds* **– winner of the Hawthornden Prize 2020, shortlisted for the Costa Poetry Award 2019**

talk to me
about when we
were perfect

talk to me about when we were perfect

amanda huggins

www.victorinapress.com

Copyright © 2023 by Amanda Huggins
First published in Great Britain in 2023 by
Victorina Press
Wanfield Hall
Kingstone
Uttoxeter
Staffordshire, ST14 8QR
England

The right of Amanda Huggins to be identified as author of this work has been asserted by her in accordance with the Copyright, Designs and Patents Act 1988.

All rights reserved. No part of this book may be reprinted or reproduced or utilised in any form or by any electronic, mechanical, or other means, now known or hereafter invented, including photocopying and recording, or in any information storage or retrieval system, without permission in writing from the publisher and/or the author.

Typesetting and layout: Jorge Vasquez
Cover design: Triona Walsh

British Library Cataloguing in Publication Data
A catalogue record for this book is available from the British Library.

ISBN: 978-1-7395801-1-7

Typeset in 12pt Garamond
Printed and bound in Great Britain by 4edge Ltd

contents

talk to me about when we were perfect	1
out chasing boys	3
at the kitchen table	5
okaeri	7
songs of leaving	9
the take-care-look-out girl	11
in the malt shovel	13
turn of the tide	15
the new knowing	17
the man in room seven	19
the vaquero's horse	21
two wild horses	23
dizzy with it	25
puncture repair kit	27
whatever speed i dared	29
saying it out loud will make it true	31
sparrow footprints	33
as though you were their own	35
pillion	37
bridgeport	39
seaside rock	41
our heavy, haloed star	43
no doubt	45
all those years, we were dancing	47
each of us a petal	49
the sound of a heart breaking	51
car by car	53
the suitable boy	55
komorebi	57
photos of friends	59
all of those boys	61
in room twenty-two	63
the ending	65
at a brighter slant	67
a ribbon of red	69
egg	71

when love was all we knew	73
in the photo booth	75
chris clarke-with-an-e	77
listing	79
london calling (part I)	81
london calling (part II)	83
the names of seaweed and collective nouns for birds	85
my twin sister	87
the light	89
today, she doesn't mind at all	91
the boundless everything	93
lunchtime, odesa	95
cat on the veranda	97
waiting for him to come home	99
some other place	101
i wasn't expecting you home quite yet	103
on hearing gerry rafferty's 'baker street'	105
drowning, falling, flying away	107
when someone you still think about messages to say hello	109
our stories	111
not quite you	113
the day you make a memorial	115
one more day with you	117
violet cream	119

For George

talk to me about when we were perfect

She can still picture his room:
walls the blue of a starling's egg,
sheets cool against her skin,
a stack of books beside his bed,
some song from the nightclub playing in her head,
asking if she'd ever fallen in love.

She remembers his mouth on her skin,
the ravel of their limbs,
but what remains of those hesitant words,
weightless as birds,
whispered shyly at first light?

Or the words mumbled as they dressed,
blushing and awkward at 6 a.m.
before they edged around his kitchen,
instant coffee scalding her tongue,
him apologetic, already late for work,
her saying nothing, wishing he would stay.

All those words drift like ghost ships now,
their beauty lost and left to rust,
yet she remembers the soft beat
of that transcendent hour,
the weight of grief when she understood
their lives would unfold in a different place.

She still thinks of him when she hears that song,
of those times he was there to save her
when the others slipped through the cracks.

And all she wants to say to him is
talk to me about when we were perfect,
because even today, she needs to know
that he once thought it too.

out chasing boys

We spent summer on the seafront,
two stranded mermaids
killing time.
We rolled up our jeans,
carried our shoes,
blew kisses at the camera
in the photo booth.
Always out, chasing boys,
as if we had forever.

In the clamour and haze
of O'Reilly's arcade,
we revered those rake-limbed lads
on the slot machines
as though they were gods,
not fishermen's lads.
And our laughter cascaded
over penny falls
as we pouted, hands on hips,
all flirt and glance,
eyes half-closed with the want
of something we didn't understand.

at the kitchen table

The late spring snow
catches us off-guard,
drifts against the henhouse wall,
blots out the distant fells.

And here, in this borrowed house,
we watch, transfixed,
brave the blizzard
to throw scraps for the birds,
half-wishing it could always be like this.

Just you and I
at the kitchen table:
a dog-eared novel,
the weekend papers,
the last bottle of wine
waiting on the shelf
until the sheep are fed.

Yet we know
the snow will thaw by morning,
and we'll drive down the lane
for bread and logs,
ice-melt from the trees
pattering on the bonnet.

Then, too soon,
the workday grind will call us back
from this adopted life
to the small house in the town,

where everything is a little less bright
and a little less kind.

As we leave,
the weather will change again,
the brilliant shine of it
making us smile,
and I'll point out a newborn lamb,
his pink ears backlit by the sun,
as he watches us drive away.

okaeri

The house is quiet now,
there's no one to call out to
when the DJ plays our favourite song,
only the rhythm of rain on glass
and the solemn tick of the kitchen clock.

How I long for the familiar sound
of your key in the lock,
your voice in the hallway
at the same time each day.
Tadaima! you'd shout. *I'm home!*

As summer wanes,
the breeze spins restless leaves,
tangles wind chimes, rattles paper screens,
and swallows take their roll call on the wire,
make ready to fly south again
with all our squandered beauty
stowed beneath their wings.

And so I wait out winter,
warm our love on a low flame,
fashion its cloak from fallen feathers,
anchor it with stones.

I whisper to you in the dark,
breathe my greeting into cupped hands,
hold it close to my ribs
in readiness for your return.
Okaeri! I'll say. *Welcome back!*

songs of leaving

There is a photo somewhere,
long since misplaced,
perhaps marking a forgotten recipe
or buried at the back of a bedroom drawer:
you, sprawled out on the picnic rug,
pale curls tangled in sunshine;
me at your side, a smile so wide, so certain.

I tasted warm beer on your lips that day,
glimpsed the end of summer
darting between copper-bright trees,
sunlight slipping slowly
behind blue-grained hills
as the band sang their songs of leaving.

And in the morning, parch-mouthed, bones
aching, clothes damp with dew,
you pulled nubs of twig, a dead moth,
the skeletons of leaves
from your hair.
Then you smiled,
and the music spun me round again
as though it had never ended.

the take-care-look-out girl

I was eleven
when I wrote my first love poem,
and I can still feel the heat
of that unrequited flame
blazing between the clichés
and the threadbare phrases.

I remember how much it burned
before it fizzled.

I saw his mother talking on the TV,
a slick of gloss across each eyelid
as green as any emerald isle.
Something caught in her throat
when she said she hoped her boy
would find a girl to take care of him,
to look out for him,
and that he'd not be taken in
by a pair of false lashes batting for gold.

I knew this take-care-look-out girl was me.

So I didn't offer up my love warily
or leave any room for doubt,
didn't ask him to read between the lines
or search for me in the crowd.
Instead, I charged in hard,
poured it out in rhyming verse,
my passion laid bare in the school magazine,
my devotion revealed for better or worse.

in the malt shovel

She sits at their familiar corner table,
the ring-marked wood scrubbed clean,
the fire all smoke and spit,
three Delft jugs still hanging from the beam.
She can picture the others, as clearly as before,
tumbling through the tap room door,
ushered inside by a blast of winter's breath,
knitted hats pulled down low.
She touches the wall above the fireplace
where he scratched their initials with a coin,
smooth now, repapered dark grey,
and the worn velvet seat replaced.
But the light is as she remembers;
the way it slants across her table,
and the background chatter,
the unwinding of scarves,
that feeling of coming home.

turn of the tide

Tow-haired lasses on piebald ponies,
soot-faced, bare-backed,
collecting sea coal in blackened sacks,
their fathers, brothers,
eyes narrowed against outsiders
as they wait for the turn of the tide.

There's those who've tried to erase this village,
pack fishermen off to inland towns
with a suitcase of curl-edged promises,
hoping to hand their cottages to city folk
who paint over the past
with Farrow and Ball.

Yet how could they leave the sea
they breathe,
eyes narrowed against outsiders
as they wait for the turn of the tide.

the new knowing

We sit side by side on the playground swings
and talk of the shine in a distant city.
Two homespun girls turned restless moths,
dancing around these northern lights,
cleaved by hope to this one-trick town
that keeps hearts and wings from heading south.

Yet there's a softness to the air tonight,
as though we've made it somewhere else—
a place more gentle, where boys whisper in Italian,
and the put-put of scooters can be heard
on a distant coastal road.

Then everything falls silent, and we know,
know for one brief moment of teenage clarity,
that life will be good and worth the wait.
We each hold the new knowing close to our ribs
and don't speak of it, just in case it isn't true.

the man in room seven

The morning is still holding its breath
when I step out across the hotel lawn,
and a breakfast party of startled crows
complain, all tut and flap and mutter.
Beyond the copse and scattered bluebells,
I discover a hidden garden,
sit down on its forgotten bench,
let myself be saved by sparrow chatter
and fountain babble,
the hum of spring's first bees.
Instead of listing all tomorrow's thankless tasks,
I idly count the panes of broken glass
in the orangery
and watch a pair of rabbits
make a dash across the grass.
All the rest can wait.

When I set off back,
I catch snatches of a distant voice,
and find the man from room seven
pacing the terrace,
talking to his office about
proaction and options and ramifications,
unable to leave it alone for even one day.
Doesn't he know
it isn't the big decisions we make
which determine life's course,
but the tiny things,
those split-second whims,
that single blink of a butterfly's wings?

two wild horses

You hear his motorbike beneath your window,
and the railings stain your palms with rust
as you tumble down the steps too fast,
scared he'll ride away before you reach the gate.
You stretch up to touch the nape of his neck,
that vulnerable inch of skin
between helmet and leather,
wondering (yet again) if he could ever love you.

Much later, when the white lines pull you home
like Theseus's thread,
you want to ride and ride and never arrive,
to gallop off the edge like two wild horses
and find that place where there be dragons.

In the service station, you roll him a cigarette,
fetch him coffee from the machine,
hold him tight a little longer
beneath the unkind light.
You know it's almost time
for the lies,
the unravelling,
the ending.

When the goodbye comes,
you tell your friends it scarcely matters,
tell yourself you won't indulge
in what-might-have-beens.
No candles will be carried,
no breath will be wasted,

you're ready to move on.
A clean break. All dusted and done.

Until that blue-white day in winter when
you pass the gallery and
cup your hands against the glass
to watch a girl hang a painting of horses.
You recall the pattern of his mother's carpet,
the tiled coffee table, her favourite picture.
You can still see that galloping stallion,
the spume and spray,
the cheap white frame scuffed at the edges.
She leaned in, her face so close to yours,
and you knew she couldn't bear
the fact that you loved him too.

dizzy with it

We wrote our songs on Saturdays,
after Chelsea Girl and the Wimpy Bar,
lyrics strewn with doodled stars
scattered across your bedroom floor.

I play-play-played those dented drums—
three cast-off cake tins of your mam's,
accompanied by the pick and strum
of your wreck-necked red guitar.

And we thought we'd go far,
we were dizzy with it.

You taped it all on your dad's reel-to-reel:
my unsure voice, your backing hum,
the dum-dum-thrum
of those battered drums
and the slip-slide-scratch of six steel strings.

We'd stop and dance to the radio, when
the DJ revealed the week's top ten,
your Bolan curls a half-crazed tangle,
and my patched-up pale-sky jeans
embroidered with all our rockstar dreams.

puncture repair kit

Through the café window
I watch a man wheel his bicycle
out of the repair shop and ride away.
For a moment there is only the smell
of glue and rubber, chalk and dust:
a puncture kit
opened up on a hot day
in the cobwebbed shed,
those scents of childhood summers
as potent as cut grass and Ambre Solaire.
I see my father's sleeves rolled up,
signifying serious intent,
the bowl of water for the inner tube,
the silence of concentration,
and me, holding my breath.

whatever speed i dared

The empty motorway carves its way west,
cuts through moor and hill,
no tail lights in front, no headlights behind,
everything uncommonly still.
Right now, I could drive
in whichever lane I wanted
at whatever speed I dared,
criss-cross the curving lines of cats' eyes,
wind down the window,
blast out 'Born to Run',
howl into the night
like an American werewolf.

Caught in my full beam,
a skittish hare makes a dash
for the other side.
He pauses for a moment,
all gold-spun fur and liquid eyes,
ears raised, one front paw held high.
I lift my own foot off the pedal,
grip the wheel, ready to swerve.
But he moves off again
without a backward glance,
leaping the barrier,
melting into darkness.

I shiver and turn the music down,
moving over to the inside lane,
slowing to sixty until headlights
appear in my rear view mirror again.

saying it out loud will make it true

You find the note on the bedroom floor,
folded into a tiny secret,
love and lust dancing
their tango on a slip of paper
no bigger than your palm.
You stare at a blonde square
of evening light reflected on the wall,
watch it fade as the sun dips,
as you listen to the call
of your unsteady heart.

When you walk into the kitchen,
your choice made,
holding her love note like a grenade,
he turns towards you,
face composed to hide the lies,
holds up his car keys, smiles,
says he's meeting a friend from work.
You want to speak,
but simply kiss his cheek
and close the door behind him,
because saying it out loud will make it true.

sparrow footprints

In those final months,
did you ever think back
to our afternoon in Kamikochi:
the warmth of the October sun,
dry twigs snapping underfoot?
I held out the skeleton of a cherry leaf,
told you autumn was proof
that death could be beautiful.

You lagged behind as we climbed the hill,
paused at the top, out of breath.
I laughed, said we were getting older,
but I remember now that you didn't reply.

We stopped at a bridge and you sat on the steps,
unfastened your boot to shake out a stone.
I crouched beside you,
watched you run your fingers
over a line of tiny footprints in the concrete.
Proof, you said, that even the smallest of us
can leave a lasting mark,
that we all live on after our beautiful deaths.

We should make a pledge, I replied,
that if we ever lose touch, we'll meet here,
ten years from today,
where the sparrow left his footprints.
It was an easy promise,
I was so sure we'd never be apart.
You looked up at the cherry trees,

and for a moment I remembered them in spring.
Then I saw the uncertainty in your eyes.
Yes, you said, quietly, we must do that.

as though you were their own

Did you ever meet your real mother and father?
the thoughtless always ask,
as though your parents were surely fake,
a hologram, somehow second best.

And yes, you agree it was a miracle
they could spare any love for you at all,
that they could bathe and change and care and kiss
and feed and bounce with endless smiles,
could cherish you and make you feel completely safe
when all the while their hearts were surely breaking
for those tiny bodies in unmarked graves.

Oh yes, the thoughtless say,
*I'm sure they loved you
as though you were their own.*

I'm sorry they don't understand
that there is no 'as though',
but I've never bothered to tell them so
until now.

pillion

He zips his jacket, fastens his helmet,
turns to say goodbye at the café door,
and the song I chose
is still playing on the jukebox,
telling him not to go.

One day soon, he'll reach for my hand
and ask me to ride pillion.
We'll take the road to Jackson's cove,
swallows sweeping low
in the violet-hemmed dusk,
our edges blurred in the slip of the sand.

I already know the ride back will feel faster
and all the girls will whisper
when we walk through the door,
that he'll order two coffees
and we'll sit with his friends,
that I'll blush when they ask where we've been.

seaside rock

I was a café racer,
all noise and speed,
you dazzled
with mirrored adornment.
I was bitter and baccy
to your purple hearts,
I was rock, roll, metal,
to your Jam, Who, Ska.

We were sworn enemies:
a Shark, a Capulet,
a Montague, a Jet,
trading our insults in the arcades
on Sunday afternoons.
Yet I held your name in my mouth
like melting ice cream,
envied the girl perched on your Vespa
with the elfin face,
hoped that one day
we might cross the wide divide,
two ill-starred lovers
wrapped in a delicious secret
behind the fortuneteller's booth.

And now our summer has taken flight,
we probably appear similar
on the surface,
to the untrained eye.
Yet at our core
we remain one or the other,

mod or rocker, rocker or mod,
and if you slice us open
you'll find those words
tattooed on our hearts,
running through our veins
like the letters in seaside rock.

our heavy, haloed star

As we drove homeward
that dull December evening,
the city lights vanished behind us,
and endless broken lines
stitched motorway lanes in place,
one by one, on and on,
leading us away
from our sometime Eden.
We sang aloud to the radio,
stolen time still carrying us high,
and when our brightness palled,
we turned to the chirp of small talk,
offered mints and bottled water,
not daring to let the car choke up
with silence
when time was running out again.
A heavy, haloed star
hung low in the winter sky,
mistaken, at first, for a plane coming in to land,
and I recalled the Angel of the North
when she first spread her wings
in the year we met.

no doubt

If I ever question my love for you,
aware that the years have wearied its shine,
knowing we can't outrun
the ravages of familiarity,
then I picture life without you.

I have you stolen by a nameless illness,
some freak accident or fall,
taken without saying goodbye.
I imagine the house
still strewn with your possessions:
the cracked, tea-stained mug I loathe,
your shaving brush left out to dry
with bristles over-splayed,
a ziggurat of half-read books,
each marked with scribbled notes,
newspaper folded open at the crossword,
waiting for you to solve that final clue.

Not forgetting those four small nails
on the kitchen table,
left there as though to vex me.

I can feel them in my hand,
weightless, featherlight,
yet sharp as loss,
and I know there is no doubt,
no question.
My grief pours out, unstoppable,
until I hear your key in the door.

all those years, we were dancing

Life presses us to the wall right now
and moments of sweetness are few,
barely enough to keep our heads
above the sapping weight of fear.
What seemed before to be a fight,
a tussle, an uphill climb,
was nothing of the kind.
All those years, we were dancing,
not marching,
yet we didn't see it at the time.
We were blind.

I want to fall in love this very moment
and never touch the ground,
to tumble down and deep like Alice
into a crazy wonderland.
I want to write down
each of those words you whispered,
then fold them tight
like the numbers in a raffle draw,
so that when I need your love the most,
I can spread it out
like a picnic on the bedroom floor.

worship
you
forever
cherish
more

eyes
      my
            take
      I
can't
      off
            you

Je t'adore
mon amour
je t'adore.

each of us a petal

(After 'In a Station of the Metro' by Ezra Pound)

Spring rain in Kyoto brings to mind
Ezra Pound's faces in the crowd,
commuters clustered like blossom petals
on his wet, black bough,
waiting on the platform at Shijo station,
quiet, tired, homeward bound.

Today, walking from Nanzen-ji,
the flower-laden trees
have brought me their early morning silence,
their stillness, their own gentle reminders
of mortality and the departed.
I contemplate our fate:
to admire the blossom's grace,
to lament its fall, to acknowledge, year on year,
everything gone and everything gathered.
Each of us a single grain of rice,
each of us a petal on a rain-splashed bough.

the sound of a heart breaking

Don't mistake the slam of a door
or a raised voice wielding careless words
for the sound of a heart about to break.
No, those are cracks, rifts, cries for help,
a rehearsal, a blip, a last hurrah,
all part of love's fierce commotion
in the fading light.

A breaking heart is something quieter,
something wrapped in the low hum
of a streetlight at 4 a.m.
It is the faint lament of a distant siren,
the chink of milk bottles
placed on an early morning step,
the lone chirp of dawn's first sparrow,
the percussion of coat hangers
quivering on an empty rail.

car by car

We locked antlers in your Triumph Stag,
all curved flanks and gleaming chrome,
pedal to the floor, engines roaring,
breaking the speed limit every night.

A year later, we coasted downhill
to a Datsun honeymoon,
Just Married scrawled in lipstick on the boot,
ten tin cans clattering in our wake.
On the way home I felt that subtle shift,
as though someone had switched to cruise control.

I endured the school runs
in my runabout Renault:
French homework unfinished,
arguments unstoppable,
la musique cranked up way too loud.
You kept phoning from the office
to say you were running late,
but by then I was running on empty.

Then I found my best friend's earring
glinting like a cat's eye
in the footwell of your Jag.
I broke down, and we broke up.

the suitable boy

How could a boy be suitable
when he'd never seen *Mean Streets*
or parked on double yellow lines?
When he hadn't read Ginsberg
or heard *Blood on the Tracks,*
had never slipped in through the out door
as the gates were padlocked at five?

When he'd never driven into woods
on a coal-dark night
to lay down his jacket beneath fistfuls of stars,
his lips so urgent you thought you might die?
When he'd never bought you
a tequila sunrise on payday
and promised you the world in its blazing sky?

The suitable boy had a Morris Marina,
wore chinos and brogues, a golf club tie,
took you for dinner at the Acropolis grill,
ordered steaks and the very best French wine.
Then he kissed you goodnight with his seatbelt on,
as if scared you might persuade him to fly.

komorebi

My heart will keep hold of that Japanese word
for dappled sunshine spilling through trees,
the interplay between light and leaves,
and it will never forget the dizziness of love
like an unending intake of breath.
Those two things alone will carry it through
the cancelled trains and relentless rain,
the loneliness of this different London,
bottles of red which never drown the pain,
lost jobs and arguments,
my team never winning,
the shows of hands, the endless votes,
which never go our way.

all of those boys

At the boating lake
we tangle oars
with shipyard boys
down for the fair.
They roll us cigarettes,
yet all we inhale
is their cheap cologne
as they kiss us quick
in the photo booth
and squeeze us slowly
behind the arcade.

At the motorcycle track
we're too fast to live,
with our Marlboro Lights
and Thunderbird wine,
taking Polaroid shots
of those lads from Leeds,
all brag and speed
on their chrome machines,
tattoos proclaiming
they're too young to die.

In the Dog and Gun
we perch at the bar,
Gauloises held high like movie stars,
and that Whitby lad
with his wide angle lens
chews gum
and looks me straight in the eye.

When the shutter clicks,
he flashes a smile,
swears blind
we could both be centrefolds.

When I look at that box of photos now,
I've forgotten dates, can't remember names,
but I still recall the smell of Brut,
of Juicy Fruit and engine oil,
and the way all of those boys made me feel.

in room twenty-two

You've left me here again
in this bland hotel, in this neutral space
which becomes our special place
one night each year,
left me here in this small square room
where we breathe more deeply,
tick more loudly,
than we could ever do elsewhere.

You've left me here in room twenty-two
with its partial sea view
and off-white sheets,
with the cheap chipped cups,
the unbranded coffee,
the plastic spoons and long life milk.

You've left me here to pace the pier,
its railings adorned with messages
from lovers lost and missed,
to trace your words with my fingertips.
*Mollie, I will return each year to be with you
for one more perfect day.*

the ending

He stood in the bathroom doorway,
his face still scrambled with sleep,
and told me that John Lennon was dead
as though it scarcely mattered.
I turned off the tap, wiped my face,
came down to listen to the radio—
five shots fired outside the Dakota
while I was quietly sleeping.

Somewhere inside me a door slammed shut,
and when he left for work, I already knew
that this death would be our ending too.

at a brighter slant

He leaves her in the heat of summer,
yet she can see the decision was made in haste,
can tell he's testing out this new life
with his boots still firmly laced.
She watches him reverse the car,
leave Golders Green for Camden Town,
finds herself yearning for a distant coast
and her familiar northern stars.

She makes a phone call to the office,
sets off to catch the 10.22,
surprised to feel relief and grief
in equal measure,
to observe they are both as true,
to see the city in a kinder light,
the sunshine at a brighter slant.
She buys a sandwich, glances at the clock,
grabs a coffee, sweetened for the shock,
then watches her old life disappear
as the train leaves platform four.

Down at the water's edge,
lulled by the cadence of the waves,
she is pleased to find
the receding tide
has swept him out to sea,
and in the Mariners Arms
she finds old friends
with whom to talk of this and that,
but she doesn't mention he has left,

doesn't speak of him at all.

Back home, there are flowers from the office,
no one having quite known what to say,
and she notices from her window
that the world is somehow wider.
She pictures him in a hazy Camden pub
with this girl who has promised the moon,
wishing only that he'd met her sooner.
And later, when his car pulls up,
she bolts her door and ignores the bell,
sits on the stairs until he's gone.

a ribbon of red

I saw you yesterday
through the barber's window,
tanned forearm resting on the counter.
Your old tattoo has been re-inked,
and a ribbon of red
runs beneath the entwined bluebirds
where my name used to be.

So you have erased me now,
just as my body rubbed out our almost-baby,
the one that slipped away from me
when her heart was still a poppy seed,
sliding out in a ribbon of red
before she even had a name to lose.

egg

I found an egg
half-hidden in the grass,
the softest blue, no bigger than a thumb nail.
You carried it to the cottage in your handkerchief,
held it up against the light,
expecting to see a half-formed bird
through the freckled shell.
A bird that would never hear the wind
or see the endless breadth of the sky,
would never swoop and soar on the currents,
see his shadow on the water
or take in the glitter of the sea and the roll of a hill
in a single dive.
Yet there was nothing to see,
only albumen and yolk,
and I realised we'd both
been holding our breath.

when love was all we knew

Grounded by the storm,
the crew from the trawler
take shelter in our cottage,
drop oilskins by the door,
drag chairs across the flags,
crowding the Aga as I pour their tea.

Never thought I'd see you back here, he says.
London, was it? The bright city lights?
And I remember his kiss behind the science block,
something malty-sweet on his breath,
the heat of his skin
through the sleeve of my blouse.
Yes, I say, *London.*

I thought the city would be mine forever
with her grit and spit and swagger,
all art and song and high kicks,
scorched summers, office windows thrown wide,
lunches at French Frank's,
drinking half-chilled wine,
falling asleep on the Northern line.
But it was only a blink, mine for a moment,
like a headlong train racing by the other way.

And I remember that school trip we took
in the last week of term
when he stole someone's hat for a bet.
We ran for our lives down the museum steps,
I lost my footing and he grabbed my wrist,

whispered something I barely heard,
each muffled word an unexpected gift.

It's good to see you again, he says now,
shaking the ocean from his hair,
a single salt-drop brushing my lips like a kiss
as he leans in close.
Was the pull of the sea too strong?

I remember him fumbling with my jeans
in the herring shed behind the Anchor,
his hot breath on the nape of my neck.
Something like that, I say
as he reaches for his tea
and catches my husband's eye across the room.

And I remember, I remember, long before London,
there was a time when love was all we knew.

chris clarke-with-an-e

I see you by the bar at Amy's wedding,
an almost-stranger in your married skin,
much taller than I thought you'd be:
my all grown up Chris Clarke-with-an-e.

The boy whose kisses stung my lips
with the tang of sherbet lemons,
sharpening my colours behind the vaulting horse.

'You're my bird for keeps', the love note said,
scrawled with a cheap dip pen
and smudged where you'd folded it too soon.

Now you call my name as I turn to go,
I feign surprise, blush as we gush our shy hellos
and you say I'm looking well.

Then we both walk away, suddenly unsure,
perhaps kept apart by things unsaid,
half-curious to know our different ending:
grown-up me and Chris Clarke-with-an-e.

listing

We were shown to the back of Margot's bistro,
seated at a table listing to the left,
and you folded a ticket from the Pompidou,
tried to wedge the unsteady leg.
Yet everything still slid around
as though we were at sea,
my knife clattering on the tiles,
your napkin fluttering to the floor.

We both said it didn't matter,
our smiles brittle as we ate overcooked sole
and yesterday's bread,
sipped wine, slightly too acidic,
not properly chilled.

And as the silence deepened,
we drank too much, too fast,
ordered a second carafe,
because it did matter after all.
Turned out we were listing too,
and what would once have made us laugh
had become something else
to which we would never confess.

I already knew that when we parted at St Pancras
you'd hug me tighter than ever before
and say how lovely it had been,
still waving goodbye as you headed for the Tube.
Yet by Belsize Park you would know
the best way to tell me it was over.

london calling (part I)

Pete's brother got married in Newcastle
two days after I turned sixteen,
to a girl from London he met through work
whose name, to my shame, I don't recall.
It was love at first sight, or so he said,
insisting said love was all they'd need,
and his mother wore an Arctic smile
with a fox fur hat,
clicked her sharp tongue
at the best man's gifts:
a copy of *London Calling*
and a box of Seabrook's crisps.
I told Pete it was the coolest thing I'd ever seen,
and his da winked at me when
I offered him a light,
held my wrist a little too long
as he leant into the flame.

london calling (part II)

One weekend that summer,
we stayed with Pete's brother,
and I seized the city's flint and spark,
grasped handfuls of her rush and speed,
so many light years from our village,
from the stink of the fishing
and the scudding skies,
from the daily call to arms
of the steelworks' tannoy.

At night we drove to Spanish City
and Pete bought us red balloons
with tails of neon feathers.
I watched his brother's wife twist
her wedding band around
her finger as the salt wind
whipped strands of hair across her face.
She gazed out at the churn of the sea,
only smiling when her balloon tugged free
and was swallowed by the sky.
On the drive back, we turned on the radio,
to hear London calling her home.

the names of seaweed and collective nouns for birds

When I saw Da's salt-licked boots,
frayed cap tossed over the peg,
I'd throw down my satchel,
punch the stiff latch
and crash through the scullery,
knowing he'd be
hauling coal from the cellar,
cheeks smudged with black dust,
strangely clumsy out of water.

The tug of the tide left him breathless
when he stayed too long on the shore,
and he lived among us only half-listening
to our landlocked talk,
always waiting to set sail again.

Sea child, he called me,
his slip of a fish,
as we dived down
to the coral beds
where mermaids sang
and jellyfish danced in puffball skirts.

Mam hoped he would turn his back on the tiller,
be coaxed ashore to the herring sheds,
be anchored down by kipper and creel.
Yet Da would never trade his fins for feet.

And when I lie awake on summer nights,
the last of the light
holding out in the western sky,
I hear him recite the names of seaweed
and collective nouns for birds.

In dreams I'm deafened
by a clamour of purple claw,
lured by a charm of oyster thief,
double-crossed by a deceit of devil's tongue,
chased by a scold of landlady's wig,
outwitted by a gaggle of dabberlocks.

Then at dawn he slides beneath the waves,
drowning with the names still on his tongue,
leaving me alone once more
to run aground without him.

my twin sister

I thought I saw my twin sister
in the nightclub queue,
flirting with the doorman,
playing to the gallery,
all limbs and shine and too-short skirt.

I'd hardly seen her since we were sour sixteen,
sullen, awkward, still learning the ropes,
always reaching for each other's throats
as she snapped at my worn down heels.
I'd hardly seen her since the night
Mam slipped away and left us both behind,
sloughing us off like two dead skins
she'd been itching to unzip.

A stab of unexpected love
prised my ribs apart with its rusty blade,
and I wondered how to say hello
to this half of me I'd preserved beneath glass
and remembered as something less sharp.
She looked across and met my gaze,
her expression
an impatient question,
then turned back to her friends with a shrug
when she realised I was no one she knew.

the light

They showed me other countries,
always talking of the light,
and I still recall flashes of fuchsia
and dozing, shuttered villas
glimpsed from windows on the morning train.

My mother, slim and tan in her cartwheel hat,
would read aloud to us from the guidebook,
suggesting the basilica, the teatro, the frescoes,
until my father called a halt for coffee.
We'd wander across the piazza,
urge shopkeepers to spread out
leather notebooks and Murano beads,
unfurl silk scarves that billowed like parachutes,
only for my mother to shake her head.

And now, in the park,
I remember petals fluttering into the villa pool,
cupping half-drowned insects in my hands
and watching them rest
a few moments in the sun
before flying away on luminous wings.

I see a woman in a hat like my mother's,
swinging the lead of an unseen dog,
and think to myself, that if she were here
we'd talk of the light,
of the gold-green light of an English afternoon.

today, she doesn't mind at all

At the station there are pools of Monday blues
beneath wet umbrellas,
indicator boards showing cancelled trains,
the announcement
of a signal failure at Golders Green.

And yet, today, she doesn't mind at all,
still smiles to herself
as she taps her foot to Babylon's beat,
because this morning that's not all there is;
this morning there is him.

This morning there is the hairline scar
above his eye, a mark like a tiny star
on his left cheek,
the cloudless appraisal of his gaze,
his mouth, almost mocking,
until it breaks into a smile.

This evening there will be a hip
pressed against hers on the dance floor,
cheap coffee back at his place
(which they'll both forget to drink),
the tangle of their discarded clothes,
the pull and rush and roar of him,
like an inland sea crashing in.

Today, tonight, he is a series of gifts
still waiting to be opened,
and until she unwraps him,

discovers the erratic stitching,
scratches, nicks and flaws,
he'll remain all of those things
which make her sing.

the boundless everything

Down at the boardwalk funfair,
beneath the helter of the skelter,
amid the waltzers' whirl and spin,
we pooled our change for teenage selfies
in the booth behind the ferris wheel,
the promise of those endless days
snagged fast on our self-conscious grins.

You girls were so pretty, and you look so young!
Oh yes we so were, and ohhhh we so do,
yet now I can see the rest of our lives,
crouched down, tucked away, hidden from view.
That was just before I met Crazy Dan,
before I failed half of my mock exams,
before Da left the house for twenty Regal
and never made it home.
And if you look again more closely,
you can find it all there in our eyes,
the fairground attractions we had still to ride
and the boundless everything we didn't yet know.

lunchtime, odesa

When he joins the queue at the tobacco kiosk,
a babushka touches his sleeve,
presses violets into his hand,
ink-dark, still damp with dew.

He recalls those distant evenings in Savransky,
the scent of woodsmoke
and the sweet vanilla of Nina's skin,
white lilacs on a table in the dacha,
tiny petals scattered on the cloth like stars.

They sat outside on midsummer nights
and watched meteorites
arcing bright across the black,
threading all their future wishes
through the spinning sky.

He lights a cigarette, heads back to work,
pauses on the stairs
as he remembers that final day:
a cat watching them from the veranda, unblinking,
Nina's hair spread out in a pool of gold
beneath his silence.

waiting for him to come home

Every night she waits for the crunch of gravel,
the stagger and stumble of footsteps,
a scratching against the wood
as he fumbles with his key.
Then the crash of the door, a muttered curse,
the weave and reel of him by the bed.
She feigns sleep, pulls the blanket over her head,
prays to a god she hardly knows,
heart thumping in her chest
like the tom-tom drum of a rabbit's foot,
signalling urgent danger.

some other place

I only saw you twice a year
when you took me down to the seafront,
my small hand shyly intertwined with yours,
my finger curled into your palm
to trace the callus at the base of your thumb.

You'd point out the street sign
each time we passed,
tell me about the other Foreshore Road in Srinagar,
and how you'd take me there when I was grown
to stay awhile on the Lake of Flowers.

We'd win candy and combs on the tuppenny falls,
then perch at the counter in Sicily Joe's,
order sundaes with sprinkles
and two chocolate flakes.
You'd look around and smile
as I squeezed your hand,
willing you not to say
that it was just like Fiore's in Rome.

And if we shared a tray of cockles,
you'd gaze across the sands
as we wiped our vinegary hands,
telling me how you'd always remember
that trip you made to Killala Bay.

Later, we'd stroll on the Marine Drive a short way,
and you'd remind me of its namesake in Mumbai
(though of course you still called it Bombay),

where the sunsets were beyond compare.

Finally, we'd climb the cliff to Hairy Bob's cave,
the warm wind tugging at my hair,
and you'd kick away condoms and tissues
as I scrambled inside.
I'd peer out at you through the rough-hewn window,
my eight-year-old heart full of joy,
because Hairy Bob's cave
never took you away
to a memory of some other place.

i wasn't expecting you home quite yet

Home early, to find the back door bolted,
to thump on the glass with the palm of my hand,
to hear something crash, footsteps on the stairs,
frantic whispers through an open window.
To push my way past you into the hall,
to see the front door swinging wide,
to glimpse a patterned scarf, a yellow coat,
disappear behind the wall.
You're early, you say,
waving your arm, as if to dismiss
what I can clearly see.
A colleague… a friend… someone I met…
I wasn't expecting you home quite yet.

on hearing gerry rafferty's 'baker street'

We explored each other, inch by inch,
in a guesthouse off the Edgware Road,
discovered London, kiss by kiss,
made it ours, and ours alone.

I thought I'd dress like Annie Hall,
write novels and smoke Sobranie Blues,
you'd paint our Hampstead floorboards white,
read poetry in the afternoons.

Yet when my time for London came,
there was no you, no teenage dream,
all that was left was the drab routine
and the long commute on the Northern line.

And each time I hear 'Baker Street',
I recall that summer, way back when
we both believed the stars were ours,
so sure we'd make it to the end.

drowning, falling, flying away

The laws of physics insist
I should be floating, not drowning,
in this salt-deep sea;
sailor not submariner.
Yet how can I surf the waves
and swim through coral gardens
when sharks are snapping at my ankles
as sirens serenade the lost?

The laws of physics dictate
I should be earthbound,
feet firmly planted,
not flying high above these clouded hills.
Yet why would I choose to be anchored down,
head half buried in the sand,
when flawed hope can pull me clear and free
into the lies of the false, wide blue?

The laws of physics state
I should be motionless at rest,
not plunging fast to certain death
from this planet's dizzy edge.
Yet how can I sit quiet and still
when so many are being slammed against the wall,
when the rest have turned their backs on truth,
mistaking endless choice for freedom?

The laws of physics say
for every action there will be a reaction,
yet have we ever come closer

to the laws of physics drowning,
falling,
flying away?

when someone you still think about messages to say hello

I thought back
to the last time we met,
to those few words exchanged
in the dairy aisle
which said something much more
than the sum of their parts
but still far less than we'd hoped.
And I thought about replying
to this new hello
with a casual invitation.
Coffee at Joe's?
A drink after work?

But I was already imagining
the stale light in a cheap hotel room,
skin on skin, bone on bone,
the rush and sing of blood,
teeth, lips, muscle.
And I already knew
the idea of it was too perfect
to ever risk letting it happen.

our stories

What will survive of us for strangers to find?
Will we leave a legacy
more visible, more lasting,
than Larkin's talk of love?
A diamond earring
dropped in the long grass,
dug up a century hence
and polished with spit
in some suburban battlefield?
Secret letters to lovers,
foxed, curled, brittle,
pored over by the couple who
stumble upon their forgotten retreat?
A prized Lobmeyr champagne bowl
sold by mistake in a mixed lot
at a house clearance sale,
chipped at the rim, the pink enamel worn thin,
yet still a heart-stopping beauty
when held up to tomorrow's light?

Or will our stories be something more prosaic?
My late father's copy of *Schindler's Ark*
surviving the endless Oxfam cycle,
the starting price still pencilled inside the cover,
or my mother's souvenir tea towels
hanging on different hooks
in basement kitchens far from here?

At the auction house
I hold up a porcelain shepherdess,

a gold fob watch,
each with a missing hand,
run my fingertips across a balding fox,
peer inside an evening bag
in the hope of finding treasure—
a theatre ticket or tortoiseshell comb
slipped into hiding through a tear in the lining.
I listen for the ghosts
of mistresses and long-dead mothers,
those gallant sons and secret lovers
whose lives are now laid bare.
For though these things are what will survive of us,
without our stories they are so much dust.

not quite you

I see you curled in the kitchen chair,
stretched out on the sun-bright ledge,
yet a second glance turns cat to hat—
a conjuring trick reversed.

Sometimes I glimpse you in the yard,
tail winding around the bins,
yet up close, there's a stripe adrift,
an extra smudge of grey beneath the chin,
an amber eye too pale,
a face too plump, too flat, too thin.

Each of these cats are not-quite-you,
a doesn't-pass-muster second best.

None have the tiny heart
that beat against my leg, as faint as a bird's,
as you slept on my lap,
so thin and frail, in your life's last days.
None have the feisty spirit
that flew from beneath your ribcage
as I pressed my hand gently into your fur
in that small, green, sterile room.
So brief a life, so brief a death,
stopped short at that last quiet breath,
yet still your fragile heart beats
some distant rhythm inside my own.

one more day with you

If I could have one more day with you,
we would wander through the Campiello,
sit in the shade of the Liston colonnade
with two cold beers
and invent the life stories
of every passer-by.

violet cream

At lunchtime I buy violet creams,
your favourite kind in the turquoise box.
We eat them in silence,
our old plaid picnic rug draped across your bed,
and I sit at your side in denial,
still sewing names tags
into clothes you'll never wear again.

I feel the rough blanket against my hand,
remember it spread out on summer Sundays,
long grass tickling my toes
and the chipped china plates stacked
with slices of buttered bread,
a quarter of thick ham,
your over-boiled eggs, yolks rimmed with grey,
and a single tomato for each of us
that tasted of sunlight trapped beneath glass.

Then afterwards, the violet creams.
Perfect you'd say,
and my father would place his hand over yours.

I carry on sewing name tags
like you used to do for me,
some insistent alarm ringing along the corridor,
and wish we could sit on that rug in the meadow,
bat away wasps, drink weak orange cordial,
just one final time.

You whisper something,

your words so fragile they hardly disturb the air,
and I press another violet cream
gently against your lips
to hold the memory there,
as though to seal your departure
with this final perfect thing.

acknowledgements

My grateful thanks go to Consuelo Rivera-Fuentes and the wonderful team at Victorina Press for making this collection happen, to Triona Walsh for yet another superb cover design, to Tee Inglewood for all her valuable insight, to Suzanne Conboy-Hill and Mark Wharton for their brilliant artwork, and to the ever-suffering Mr L.

credits

A number of poems in this collection were previously published by Maytree Press in the author's chapbook *The Collective Nouns for Birds,* and 'songs of leaving' and 'at the kitchen table' first appeared in the Maytree anthologies *Green Fields* and *The Cotton Grass Appreciation Society*. An earlier version of 'the new knowing' formed part of the Northern Poetry Library's 'Poem of the North', and a previous version of 'sparrow footprints' was first published by *Arc Magazine*. 'talk to me about when we were perfect', 'whatever speed i dared' and 'the boundless everything' first appeared in Issue Five of *Northern Gravy*.

illustration credits

Thanks to Suzanne Conboy-Hill for permission to use her painting 'the day you make a memorial', which was inspired by a scene "at the vet's surgery where an elderly couple waited with their dog for that final goodbye" and incorporates phrases from the author's poem 'not quite you', and to Mark Wharton for the commissioned pen and ink collage, 'Bridgeport'. 'The Vaquero's Horse' and 'Cat on the Veranda' are the author's own artwork. All interior and cover photographs © Amanda Huggins.

about the author

Amanda Huggins is the author of the novellas *All Our Squandered Beauty* and *Crossing the Lines*, as well as four collections of short stories and a poetry chapbook. Her fiction and travel writing have been widely published in national newspapers, magazines and journals, and three of her short stories have been broadcast on BBC radio. She has won numerous awards, including three Saboteur Awards for poetry and fiction, the Colm Toibin International Short Story Award, the H E Bates Short Story Prize and the British Guild of Travel Writers New Travel Writer of the Year Award. She was also a runner-up in the Costa Short Story Award and the Fish Short Story Prize, and has been shortlisted for the Bridport Prize, The Alpine Fellowship Award and many others. Amanda lives in Yorkshire and is an editor and publishing assistant.